AMSTERDAM

English edition

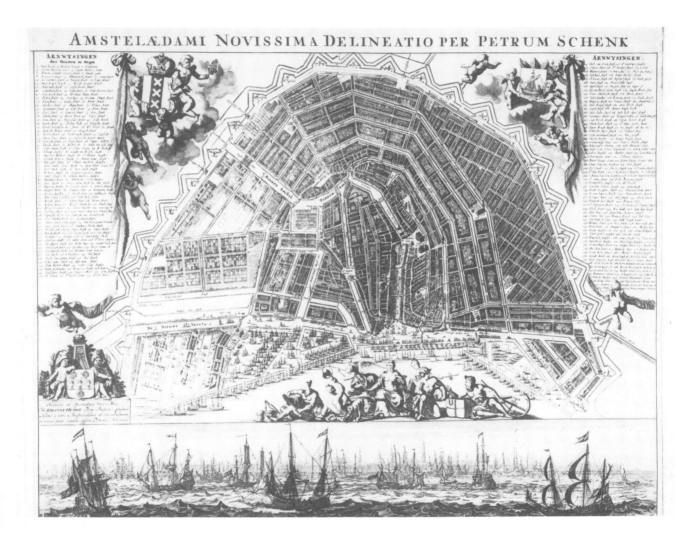

Max Dendermonde - Herman Scholten

Copyright:
Uitgeverij Van Mastrigt en Verhoeven B.V.,
Postbus 176,
6920 AD Duiven

Text: Max Dendermonde
Coördination and photographs: Herman Scholten
Other pictures:
'Historisch-topografische Atlas van het
Gemeentearchief van Amsterdam', page 1
Aerophoto Schiphol: page 4, 19, 30, 40 and 41
World View/Fototheek: page 7, 17, 34, 50/51, 67, 83, 88
Beeldbank en Uitgeefprojekten: page 10, 36, 46, 49, 53,
55, 68, 76, 87
KLM Aerocarto: page 64 and 65
Archief Rijksmuseum: page 45
Reclamedienst Nederlandse Spoorwegen:
page 5 and 91 (below)
Picture box: page 8 and 9
N.L.R. page 94

Printing:
Tamminga Siegers b.v.,
Nieuwgraaf 300,
6921 RS Duiven

Lithography:
Nederlof Repro, Heemstede

CIP-GEGEVENS KONINKLIJKE BIBLIOTHEEK, DEN HAAG

Dendermonde, Max
Amsterdam / [text] Max Dendermonde ; [coord. and
photographs] Herman Scholten ; [transl. from the Dutch].
- Duiven : Van Mastrigt en Verhoeven. - Ill., foto's
1e dr.: 1988.
ISBN 90-73296-06-4
NUGI 672
Trefw.: Amsterdam ; fotoboeken.

INTRODUCTION

To start with, there are two features which make Amsterdam such an incomparable city. The first one is the simple, though bewildering, attractive town plan, that consists of circles instead of squares. The second is the size of the area involved, which just is not too big and certainly not too small to be enjoyed by a keen walker.

That is why Amsterdam in a very natural, harmonious way still belongs to the pedestrian. In the original inner city, which was designed around 1612 and realised after that in three phases, – Herengracht, Keizersgracht and Prinsengracht –, every stranger will feel at home within a day, as if embraced by them.

The splendour of that round, encircling inner city owes itself to the fact that there are no uninteresting corners. The pedestrian, whichever way he goes, will always remain fascinated, because he will find a rich variety of beautiful houses from the seventeenth or eighteenth century, small cosy pubs, large and small shops: department stores or one-man businesses, boutiques with novelties, old shops with valuable antiques and big and small museums.

Every now and then the sightseer stops, because the city offers different surprising scenes: a barrel organ, on the bridges fishmonger carts selling herring and onions, an artist painting the most beautiful, wobbling mirrored images of the canals, a group of street-musicians and even acrobats in the summertime.

Moreover the pedestrian can find places to eat to suit any budget, some of them opening up very early in the morning while others offer their hospitality well after midnight. In Amsterdam a real pleasure seeker can find a cosy place almost any hour of the day. Amsterdam never sleeps, or hardly ever.
When the stranger walks back to his hotel in the small hours – when the sun rises rosy over the nearly quiet city – he will see what the Frenchman Jean Francois Regnard already noticed in 1681: "This city seems to be double: one can also see it in the water: and the reflection of these distinguished houses in these canals makes this spot a fairy land".

For those who sooner or later become tired walking, after all these impressions, there is excellent public transport, consisting of a tight network of tramlines, that was electrified at the beginning of this century, just when Amsterdam was having a new flourishing period, in which the inhabitants were busy again enlarging their imperial city: concentric again, thus continuing building according to the town plan of 1612. This building has been continued ever since: not only in the beginning of the century, but also after the First World War, in the twenties when Amsterdam celebrated a long summer spell (in 1928) when it was an Olympic City and a large, modern quarter was built round the new stadium. Architects from all over came to see how the Amsterdam people dealt with the "new building".
Later hotels were built there, still within reach from the inner city by a good walker.

However: the city extensions built after the Second World War are too remote from the centre, even for a good walker. No need to despair: besides the many trams there are countless buses as well as metro-lines. Of course there are always taxis: hundreds of them, day and night.

However we advise you – provided you are staying in the inner city – to keep walking, if you can keep it up. That way you will see more. If you look up for instance, you will discover the continuing exposition of splendid, classic gables, sometimes above modern shop windows. Because you can see Amsterdam at least at three levels: as a reflection in the canals, as a particularly lively city at eye-level and as a "heavenly surprise" when you look up.

All these aspects – and many more – you will find presented in detail and described on the following pages. Indeed they are not meant specifically as a manual for the sightseer, anyone can use the book as a reference while walking. The visitor can then see in reality, what the book has to offer.

It turned out a nice book, we are proud of it. However we know beforehand that in "Groot Mokum", (as the Great City has been called in Yiddish since Rembrandt's time) the reality of the city surpasses the art of any printed matter.

Why?

Because Amsterdam promoted and still promotes reality to Art.

Amsterdam is and will remain the city of beauty and the art of living!!

Our sight seeing trip depicted by photographs and description starts at the most famous railway station in the Netherlands, the Amsterdam Central Station, which has a moving history. The impressive building dates from the end of the last century when Amsterdam was a flourishing harbour city. At that time the quays and docks showed a busy and lively picture throughout the whole year: clouds of steam and sparkling white sails defined the "IJ".

Until that time water had always been the most important means of transport for the Netherlands and for Amsterdam as well. Then the Netherlands had a time-table for example for passenger boats – canal boats – that departed and arrived almost on the dot. Amsterdam wanted the old and new means of transport – thus boats and trains – to run in conjunction with one another.

Central Station and in the foreground the North-South Holland Coffee-house

A railway station adjacent to the harbour was the logical conclusion to this train of thought. It was only in 1876 that the plans for a station at the top of "Damrak" finally materialised. In the "IJ" three large, entirely artificially made islands were built. On the middle island the "Central Station" was erected, based on no less than 8687 piles with a length of no less than 20 meters each. The actual building was not just that simple, the work was delayed considerably because of subsidence. However the work was completed in 1889, exactly according to the design of the neo French Gothic style – by P.J.H. Cuypers, who designed many churches as well as the "Rijksmuseum". The "Central Station" has been changed continuously according to new demands. One of the last alterations involved the modernisation of the hall of the station.

Detail of a facade

Hall of Central Station

North-South Holland Coffee-house

One of the most famous coffee houses in Amsterdam is situated directly in front of the "Central Station". When the surroundings of the station were renovated, the original coffee house (which served as a waiting room for the boat passengers) was torn down. After that it was rebuilt to its former glory.

"Wailing Tower"

Damrak ▲ ▶

It is a splendid starting point for a trip through the city. You can make a trip, not only by foot, but also by a canal touring boat, of which there are many in Amsterdam. Near the station (see photograph below) many centuries are brought together. In the shadow of the "St. Nicolaas Church" (dated 1888) lies a semi-circular, brick building that is called the "Schreierstoren" (Wailing Tower) dating from the Middle Ages. Legend has it that it was here the wives of the seamen parted from their seafaring loved ones. What would a city be without these tales?

't Kolkje

On "Dam" square you can see two famous Amsterdam buildings at a glance: the "Royal Palace" which was completed in 1655 and the "Nieuwe Kerk" (without a tower) that dates from 1490 in its present form. The considerable amount of money designated for the tower was eventually spent to finish the palace some 150 years later. The first piles of a total of 13659 to support the palace, were driven into the ground in 1648. The foundation stone was laid in the same year. After that a heated argument started between the designer, architect and painter Jacob van Campen and the town builder Daniel Stalpaert (who was also a painter) about the building while under construction. At that time it was intended to be a townhall. The town council had a dilemma, as to whether a church tower, worthy of such a fine church, should have priority over the townhall. However, the very same town council was looking desperately for accommodation in 1652 when the old townhall burned down. In 1655 the mayor was able to take up residence in a part of the enormous new townhall.

"de Dam"

New Church

The former fishing village of "Amstellerdam" – later called Amsterdam – was already growing at such a rate that one Catholic Parish was not sufficient. At the beginning of the fifteenth century (in 1408) it was essential to found a second parish, as the "Old Church" was getting too small. At that time the building of the "New Church" had started. This church was just finished when it was destroyed by fire, a disaster that often occurred in those days. A second big fire (in 1421) caused more damage to the church. After a long period of rebuilding, which was completed in 1490, the church was struck yet again by fire for the third time. Meantime, in 1578, the Catholic possession had changed hands to the Reformed Church and to them this house of God was of the greatest importance as well, in an ever growing Amsterdam. They urged the rebuilding on, and in 1648 the "New Church" was consecrated by them.

Feeding pigeons on "de Dam"

Birds of different feathers from far and wide gather on "de Dam" square (left) to feed the legendary pigeons there. Although, in a way, they are a great nuisance because of their large numbers, they are spoiled by young and old alike.

Behind the palace the Amsterdam way of life is no less interesting. The "Raadhuisstraat", with its modernised tram-system (which dates from the previous century, at that time horse-drawn) leads to one of the most typical Amsterdam quarters, the working class "Jordaan". This area is situated – as the Jordaan song tells you – at the foot of the "Old Wester": the tower of the Western Church, where Rembrandt lies buried.

Raadhuisstraat

Singel nr. 7

A very pleasant way to get a quick impression of Amsterdam, but in a fast and comfortable way, is to take a trip in a canal touring boat with their usual informative guide. These guides speak French, German and English – apart from Dutch – and sometimes they are even capable of expressing themselves in a fifth or sixth language. They have an extensive knowledge of Amsterdam and they consider it an honour to tell tourists about their attractive city.

They have a number of musts on their programme, like the remarkable house on Singel number 7 for instance, that is traditionally mentioned as the narrowest and smallest house in Amsterdam.

The round building on the photograph on the left was completed in 1671 and is called the "Round" or "New Lutheran Church". Forty years before that an old Lutheran church was built on an entirely different site (on the corner of Spui and Singel), on the premises of the old warehouse "De Vergulde Pot". It was here, in a somewhat unobtrusive area, in a so-called "hidden church" where the German Lutherans held their secret services for a long time. In 1578, when Amsterdam changed from Spanish and Roman rule to the camp of the rebellious house of Orange and the Reformed faith, these Lutherans immediately installed a minister. After that the Catholics were looking for "hidden Churches" as their own churches had all been taken over.

It took the Amsterdam people years to get used to the terrible bollards showing the St. Andrew's Cross, the Amsterdam coat of arms. They were designed to keep all motor vehicles under control. In Amsterdam one had to make a choice: cut through the city on a large scale (which happened in some places) or show respect as much as possible for history. The latter gained the majority. Each year the number of cars increases and so does the number of "Amsterdammertjes". Amsterdam would not be Amsterdam if one did not have a humorous way with them. One turned negative into a positive. One can obtain "Amsterdammertjes" as a souvenir everywhere, even chocolate ones at a baker's.

Haarlemmersluis

The "Brouwersgracht" owes its name to the many breweries that were established here during the sixteenth and seventeenth centuries. The barley needed in those breweries, was stored in large warehouses called "spijkers" at that time. ("Spijker" means granary). In 1612 the "Brouwersgracht" was extended to the "Lijnbaansgracht". The stone tablet shown in the picture on the left can be found on the warehouse in the lower photograph and the stone tablet on the right belongs to the warehouse in the picture next to it. The "Brouwersgracht" is part of the former working class area "de Jordaan", (dating from 1612) that found its origin as an area for French immigrants (Huguenots).

Brouwersgracht

Brouwersgracht

During the nineteenth century the area pauperised by overpopulation (through dock workers from the fast growing harbour activities), and it was only after World War II that the problems in this area were slowly dealt with. It was a much loved, romantic area – a town within a town –, that boasted it's own songs and special humour.
The Netherlands Folks Stage made good use of it, and many novels have been written about it. The area is still very popular, especially with intellectuals and artists, and all kinds of Bohemians, who prefer the freedom of a house-boat to life ashore. There are many pubs and restaurants, and many people come from outwith the area, also attracted by the charming markets.

In 1624, three islands, the "Realeneiland", "Bickerseiland" and "Prinseneiland" were made and big and small wharves, warehouses and storerooms were built on them. Different industries were established as well. "Prinseneiland" (the smallest of the three) was intersected by the "Galgenstraat" (Gallow Street), which derived its name from the fact that it gave a good view of the gallows that were erected on "Volewijk" on the other side of the "IJ". To lift heavy loads into the warehouses one used a "windas" (windlass) instead of a crane, the last sample of an Amsterdam windlass can be seen in the so-called "tar-garden" of this island. A tar-garden was a piece of land where tar-buyers held their trade. "Prinseneiland" probably named after the principal building "The Three Princes" (Willem, Maurits and Frederik Hendrik) still offers the splendid view of the Amsterdam of the sixteenth and seventeenth century.

Zandhoek

The character of Amsterdam as a harbour town changed completely after the depression during the thirties, and especially after World War II. The warehouses, many of which date from the Golden Age, are not needed nowadays, but fortunately they have not been demolished.

Zandhoek ▼

They have been splendidly adapted to dwelling houses. Those who live here, feel priviliged in their cosy quarters. They maintain the old gables and are reflected in the romance of ages past.

Brouwersgracht

Why do the Amsterdam canals not smell? Not even on a sweltering summer's day? You can only find out during the night, when a very observant person will notice the water in the canals flowing. The flow is not very fast, but it is sufficient to keep the canals clean. The nocturnal flushing is regulated by the Town's Water Office and this was housed in 1878 in the "Montelbaanstower" which until a few years before that, – officially – was part of the Amsterdam defence works. A number of years before that, a new law did away with the defence works. In many a town demolition took place, to create room for growth: the age of steam burst and hissed out of its seams, the growth of the towns was enormous.

"Montelbaanstower"

The building on "Oude Schans" was kept. It dates from 1512, and the spire from 1606. *"Montelbaanstower"*
Right under – on "Lastage" – the famous ships that brought prosperity during the
seventeenth century, were built. It was absolutely necessary to have these ships yards
heavily guarded, the Spaniards were lurking. Only three years later (in 1609), the
Dutch achieved a cease-fire with Spanish enemies that was kept for twelve years.
However, it was only in 1648, with the "Peace of Munster" that the Low Countries
achieved peace. The ship yards moved to wider spaces, and the area of the "Oude
Schans" became the beautiful residential area (see above) it still is today.

Like so many churches in Europe the Amsterdam "Old Church" has much more to offer than what one would expect at first sight. The church really is a collection of churches, a collection through the centuries. Because through the centuries this beautiful building has been renovated and changed continuously. It started as a small cross shaped church that was consecrated in 1306 in a small town in the Middle Ages, in reality it was just a large village.

View from "Old Church"

It was named after "St. Nicolaas", the patron saint of the seafarers, though the name of the patron saint is seldom mentioned here now. The ties with the seafarer however have not been broken altogether: the "Oudekerksplein" has been part of Amsterdam's notorious "red light district" for years and years, where originally foreign sailors tried to find what they could not bring from their home ports! The present tower was completed during the time of the early Renaissance, in 1566, and nearly a hundred years later one of the most pretty chimes in the Netherlands was installed. Besides, there are some older bells amongst these chimes made by François Hemony.

Interior "Old Church"

Above the former "Country's Sea Store", now quite appropriately – accomodating the "Dutch Shipping Museum". On the island of "Oostenburg", the "East Indian Company" used to have extensive grounds during the "Golden Age", large wharves and fabulous warehouses. The "East Indian Company" used to manage many ships going to the East Indies, and many of those were built here under their own management. Czar Peter had a very good look round here to introduce the art and craft to his own homeland with little success though, because he was lacking what the Dutch had, namely being situated on a sea rich in trade. Because of this flourishing trade the Netherlands have always been open to the world, and this can still be seen, because the Low Countries play host to many people from various far away countries.

Maritime Museum

It was mostly the Jewish merchants that determined the spirit of the Amsterdam markets. One of the most famous markets, the one on "Waterlooplein" had to be moved temporarily to a different location, when on that square, the unique combination of a theatre and a townhall was built. This combination of buildings and ideas cannot be thought of without involving the history of the place on "Dam Square", that used to be the townhall of Amsterdam until 1808. In that year it was claimed by Louis, King of France and Napoleon's brother. The Town Council then moved to the old "Prinsenhof".

Market on "Waterloo Square"

At the beginning of this century, the first plans of an entirely new townhall were made. Meantime there were also plans for a large opera-building. The continuing uncertainty of the two seperate plans gave architect Holzbauer the idea to combine both plans. The authorities approved the plans, but the Amsterdam people only believed in them, when the 3075 foundation poles were driven into the marshy grounds and the townhall appeared. Nowadays the interior functions so perfectly, that the whole town takes pride in this unusual building. However,

the appearance still causes debates amongst the Amsterdam people. Maybe through time the facade will be regarded as beautiful, like the original Catholic building shown in the background, the Moses and Aaron Church, whose detested classism is now appreciated. It no longer serves as a church, but survives as a monument. You will find this church on Waterloo Square, that still has an interesting market (although on a smaller scale), but it is less interesting than before 1940, when Jewish humour dominated.

Townhall - Opera - Blauwbrug

The bicycle came during a period in which Amsterdam grew once again: at the end of the nineteenth century. Though to the thousands of workers in Amsterdam – that used to walk to their jobs – the bicycle was a luxurious possession for the rich at first – the bicycle and working population got along nicely together. Before the beginning of World War I (in 1914) Amsterdam was already a real cyclist town and the streets running along the canals where there were no tram-lines – seemed to have been made for cycling. Soon covered bicycle sheds were built, especially in the working-class areas, which enabled the owners to "park" their means of transport. On the whole, as a rule, until 1930 – when poverty struck through the great financial depression in those years – one could leave his bicycle unguarded anywhere, sometimes provided with a lock.

During those crisis years that changed. Many jobless were hunting for unguarded bicycles to sell them on the abundance of Amsterdam markets. When the German occupation army seized Dutch bicycles everywhere

during the last years of the Second World War it did not improve their popularity. They took one of the most cherished possessions of the Dutch. Now there are so many bicycles in Holland and Amsterdam especially, that many consider a bike as public property. The "borrowing" of an unguarded bike is so common that the police hardly intervenes. Do enjoy a bicycle in Amsterdam, if you master the art, but include a couple of locks in your purchase!

You will find boats everywhere in the Amsterdam canals, sometimes even three alongside each other. Many serve as means of transport, others have been transformed to living quarters. The Amsterdam Town Council finds it a very difficult task to control the number of people living on boats, because people with a low income cannot easily find accomodation ashore. Not all occupants of houseboats prefer a floating house for that reason alone, it often gives them a feeling of freedom. And often this feeling goes along with lightheartedness and one turns the boat into floating gardens. If one heaves the anchor, one can get sudden surprises. The water in the Amsterdam canals is a kind of cloak of love: a lot has disappeared under it! Bicycles for example!

◀ *Theater Carré*

The location of the enormous Stopera-complex has been extremely well chosen, in one of the oldest parts of the town. On a central site along the "Amstel", the river that lent it's name to the Dutch capital. Seen from the air, the complex (in the middle of the picture) improves in beauty, at least in symbolic strength. The squarish, fortresslike offices of the town council encircle and protect the curves of the art building. This is typical for Amsterdam, where the successive authorities always have been good to art and the artists. Writers, painters, musicians, actors and filmers feel more free in libertine Amsterdam than in any other city.

Stopera

Without any doubt the tower of the "Zuiderkerk" is one of the most beautiful ones of Amsterdam. It is only because of its height that this tower looks like other towers in Amsterdam. However this tower as it is now, was there in 1614. That was three years after the first Whitsun service when the church had just been finished. A Reformed service naturally. Strange as it may seem, the population gave this church a Catholic name: "St. Janskerk" (Church of St. John). The Reformed City Fathers expressed objections. After all this was the first church built by people of the Reformed faith. The building should have been called "Zuiderkerk" and gradually the name was changed. The church is located in an old part of the city that has been well preserved. If you stand on the bridge that spans the "Groenburgwal" and look towards the tower, you feel as if you are living during the flourishing times of the Low Countries.

Zuiderkerk
A.D. 1614

Catboat on "Singel"

To live in a house-boat in Amsterdam is a way of life, that makes necessity a virtue, even an art. It seldom happens that people in the lap of luxury, choose to live on a house-boat. One can find an abundance of house-boats all over the country – along the many lakes in Holland – serving as second homes and for recreation purposes.

Sarphatikade

The house-boats in Amsterdam are mainly used as living quarters. They have been there for a long time, but the big increase took place after World War II, when there was a lamentable housing shortage. Tens of thousands of home-seekers were on a waiting list for years. One also needs a licence to live on a boat in Amsterdam. That licence was easely obtained – if one had the means to buy a boat – but there were not enough berthes. Nowadays one does not need to live on a boat. One can make a choice for a life of freedom.

House-boats on Amstel

The tower of the former "Mint" is a beautiful one, originally a gate to the town (the "Regulierspoort"), when the town was much smaller. Since 1672 it served as a factory for golden and silver coins for only a few years, however the name has been maintained. The Minttower is located on a complicated crossroads for trams, cars, cyclists and pedestrians. On the left the "Reguliersbreestraat" that leads towards the entertainment centre called "Rembrandtplein". The "Kalverstraat", that used to be most important pedestrian street in Amsterdam, connects "Mint Square" and the "Dam".

Reguliersbreestraat

Rembrandt Square

"Rembrandt"

"Thorbecke"

The Netherlands have a tremendous number of sun-seekers, more than any other country, who occupy the most "sacred" places on warm days, like the public garden on "Rembrandt Plein". Rembrandt ignores it, he has eternity on his mind. The poet Vondel is less known in other countries. His name was used for a splendid public park: everything possible under the sun is tolerated here. On a warm day in Amsterdam one can sit outside anywhere one chooses. The terrace in the Dutch capital is at least as popular as any in Paris.

Amsterdam is without any doubt one of the most charming cities of the world. That is because a lot of things happen on the rather limited area of the inner city. Another reason is the beauty of the architecture and because Amsterdam is so full of life and of an outstanding floweriness, not only in the language of the people and the way they dress but also more directly by the many flower stands everywhere. On the "Singel", not far from the "Mint", there is a flower market every day, part of it is floating.

Flower market

Singel

At a number of certain places in Amsterdam one can buy tickets for a cruise through *Rokin*
the city. There are different routes. The boat shown above sails from a historical spot.
The river "Amstel" stops dead against a concrete wall, beyond are the filled-up waters
of "Rokin", that used to be a "waterway", like so many other streets in Amsterdam.
(Especially in the "Jordaan" quarters a lot of canals were filled in, around the turn of
the century.) In the thirties the last bit of the "Amstel" was filled-up as well, in spite of
a lot of protest. Amsterdam was crowded by taxis and traffic became a great problem.
Nowadays people are waterminded again: one finds a watertaxi often faster in town
than a four-wheeled vehicle (see page 79).

Not far from the "Rokin", on "Spui", one finds a small passage to a special part of Amsterdam: the "Begijnhof", a small, beautiful, open air museum where people actually live, that dates from 1346, when Amsterdam was still a Roman Catholic city.
A rich man, Coppe van der Lane, donated a piece of land to the Beguines. Beguines were devout widows or old spinsters who preferred to live in a religious community without taking the vow. After the Reformation of the sixteenth century the

Begijnhof

Protestant Amsterdam community showed their tolerance and the Catholic ladies were allowed to keep on living in their own public enclosure. Even today the "Begijnhof" serves more or less its old purpose. There are other courts in Amsterdam to be found, though most of them serve other purposes, like housing students. The one who wants to live on his own in historical premises, like the house shown above, has to pay a lot.

Begijnhof

People without cars, are doing well in Amsterdam, at least in the down-town area. A healthy Amsterdammer can walk in one hour from end of town to the other. An outsider has a little more difficulty achieving this, because there are a lot of distractions to deal with. He will often stop to look at a gable, or to take in a surprising view of the city, for instance where a number of canals meet, as shown above. There are also many tempting cafés's. He will encounter the latter especially on the unique "Leidseplein" and surrounding area, where one can find over fifty entertaiment places of completely different kinds.

Leidsestraat

Leidseplein

Without any doubt the "Leidseplein" is one of the most important cultural centres in Amsterdam. Until a couple of years after World War I that privilege was reserved solely for "Rembrandtplein" and surroundings, where there were intimate theatres and modern cabarets. But during the depression years the "Leidseplein" with its literary café's and with the "Stadsschouwburg" (seen above) and many meeting places for artists (amongst others Hotel Americain) distinctly became the centre. Gradually, especially after World War II, the narrow Leidsestraat became a favourite shopping centre, and certainly when it was declared a pedestrian precinct. Only trams are allowed to run there now.

Stadsschouwburg on Leidseplein

The famous Amsterdam "Rijksmuseum" is over a 100 years old. The contents are of such importance to Amsterdam (and the whole world) that the exterior of the building has been accepted for what it is since it was built in 1885. At that time the building was strongly criticised, because it was supposed to breathe too much of a Catholic atmosphere. It was designed by P.J.H. Cuypers, the Catholic architect who also designed the Central Station, amongst other buildings. The contents of the museum are of a great variety and extremely valuable. Nearly everyone knows that Rembrandt's "Night Watch" is on display here. It is one of the many masterpieces of the great Dutch painter.

Rijksmuseum

Nightwatch

In the immediate vicinity of the "Rijksmuseum" you will find the "Stedelijk Museum" (mainly modern art) and the modern "Van Gogh Museum", that has an ample collection to justify its name. In this "Museum Quarter" one also finds the "Concertgebouw" (see page 48) and there are two old, but revived shopping streets: the "P.C. Hooftstraat" and the "van Baerlestraat", which together form a very important centre.

Many fine restaurants and cafe's are there and the "fine fleur" of fashion. The area behind the "Concertgebouw", favoured by musicians, has become popular with other artists and intellectuals during the last few decades.

Rembrandt

It is not quite possible to compare Amsterdam with Vienna, by far **the** city of music. The latter has given us many more internationally famous composers. But since Amsterdam became a mainly democratic working class city after the middle of the last century, (exactly like Vienna) the music turned to the streets on a large scale, with brass bands in the parks, singers in the pubs in the "Jordaan", buskers and the music of the "Salvation Army" and barrel-organs and an annual "Prinsengracht" concert that is given during the evening on the spheric flood-lit "Prinsengracht".

Prinsengrachtconcert

Amsterdam is a city bursting with music. When, because of the leisure time culture in the Low Countries, the citizens needed more artistic events, the classical art turned to the streets more often. There are always new happenings, too many to mention. There is music everywhere in Amsterdam, especially during the summer.

◀ *Leidseplein*

"Jordaan"

Leidseplein

Concertgebouw

Amsterdam once (in 1986) was proclaimed the cultural Capital of Europe. After a long period of decline at the beginning of the nineteenth century Amsterdam has re-established itself since 1888. At that time the "Concertgebouw" was opened on the edge of town, three years after the "Rijksmuseum". As the eye of the Museum was dedicated to the past, the ear of the "Concertgebouw" was concentrating on the future. The soon famous Concertgebouw Orchestra – since 1895 conducted by world famous Willem Mengelberg – opened its doors to the modern composers of that time. Ravel, Debussy, Reger and so it went on, year after year.

Detail of facade

When Willem Mengelberg celebrated his 25th jubilee in 1920, there was an impressive Mahler celebration in the concertgebouw. Many a person looks back on that year dedicated to Mahler, as one of the best years in the history of cultural Amsterdam. The "Concertgebouw" has been host to many great conductors, some of them of Dutch nationality. One of those, Bernard Haitink, became world famous and it was he, amongst others, who not only retained the fame of the orchestra, but even added to it.

"Concertgebouw Orchestra"

Boats on the beach - 1888

Self-portrait

The famous Dutch painter Vincent van Gogh died when he was 37. Although he died while still young (in 1890) he really developed painting in his thirties. His best period was even in his last, particularly his two last years, in which he literally painted as if possessed. He was born on the 30th of March, the son of a preacher in Zundert, a village in one of the southern provinces of the Netherlands. Before trying to follow in his father's footsteps, he worked in the art business in Londen. Next he tried teaching in Ramsgate in England, but that was not succesful either.

Farmer's wife binding corn - 1889

Fields of Maraichea - 1889

He studied theology for a few months in Amsterdam, became an evangelist in the "Borinage", at the time a poor mining district in the south of Belgium, where he shared in the misery of his fellow people. It was because of this attitude – too little decorum – that he was fired. He was nearing his thirties when he decided to become a painter. To achieve this he had lessons from A. Mauve, a famous Dutch painter of the "The Hague School". Later he studied at the academy of Antwerp. It was only in 1886 that his work got his own, so personal touch, when he was taken care of by his brother Theo, in Paris. This brother had quite a blooming art trade there. Theo supported Vincent, financially as well. The two brothers kept up a lively correspondence. That's how we know so much about the evolvement of Vincent. In 1888 he arrived in the south of France, where he lived for some time in a hotel in Arles. The strong sun (and Mistral winds) stimulated his working power enormously.

Self-portrait

Sometimes he did four paintings in just one day. When he realised he was exceeding the limits of sanity, he went for treatment to Cachet, a neurologist in the Village of Auvers-sur-Oise, where in the end, he committed suicide. Almost his entire works became the property of his supporter, his brother Theo. "The Netherlands" benefitted greatly from this, as the van Gogh family donated most of this property to two important Dutch museums, of which one is located in Amsterdam, the modern, now world-famous van Gogh Museum, in the museum quarter behind the equally famous "Rijksmuseum".

Especially, after 1960, when prosperity increased enormously in the Netherlands, and almost every town needed labourers, hundreds of thousands of foreigners, especially from Mediterrannean countries, flocked to the Low Countries. Amsterdam did not have to become accustomed to them. In the hospitable city the people were used to all kinds of strangers: British Protestants (some of which later set sail from Leiden to America on the "Mayflower"), German anabaptists and Morovian Brothers, Polish and Portuguese Jews, French Huguenots, men and woman from Java or Sumatra and German immigrants after 1933 etc. The outline in Amsterdam, and especially the look of the many martkets, has been largely enriched by the exotic influences, not in the least by all the new food. The rather simple, originally farmlike Dutch cuisine has been changed drastically because of this.

Albert Cuyp Market

"Free Market"　　　　　　　　　　　　　　　*Flower Market Amstelveld*

Amsterdam has many varied day markets. The long, nowadays so exotic "Albert Cuyp" is always mentioned first, but there are more, like the "Wester Market" (also famous), and the "Lindengracht" (on Saturdays), the "ten Kate Market", and the "Vespucci Market" in the West of Amsterdam, in the Jan Evertsen area. We did not mention them all by far. A very important market is the "Free Market", on April 30th, when the Dutch celebrate their Queen's birthday. On that particular day, the whole of Amsterdam is the scene of one big market. All citizens are allowed to sell their surplus goods everywhere in the streets. This is done on a large scale, and the city looks very festive – with all the music and food-stalls.

Waterlooplein Market

On the edge of the "Jordan" on the opposite side of the "Prinsengracht" is the most talked about (and even sung about) building in Amsterdam, the tower of the "Westerkerk", that was consecrated in 1631. The population of the "Jordan" that used to sing that they were living "at the foot of the old Wester" always considered the "Westertoren" as theirs. The building is a creation by the hand of the great architect "Hendrick de Keyser", who did not live long enough to see the work completed. He died ten years before the consecration of the church. His son, working along with foreman bricklayer Cornelis Danckerts, continued the work. The famous tower was finally completed in 1638. It is 85 metres high and fascinates every connoisseur of the building trade, because, in spite of the Renaissance-like style of de Keyser, so many Gothic motives have been used.

Amsterdam has hundreds of bridges, very old ones, and very modern ones. These too have a character of their own in Amsterdam (see page 38) because progressive architect Piet Kramer gave his advice for the building of new bridges from 1917 on. He applied wrought iron works and gave sculpturers – amongst them Hildo Krop – a great influence and part in the job. It is written that because of this, the bridges often acquired something "Monumental" or "Royal".

*Panorama from
Westerkerk*

Anne Frank House

Something imperial we would say. One could make more small similés like that in Amsterdam. For exemple the similé between the house on "Prinsengracht" number 263 and the "Westerkerk". Between the young girl who used to "live" at this address and the old man buried in the "Westerkerk". The chimes of the "Westertoren" made a connnection between these two persons. The young girl listened to it for more than two years, when she was hiding from the German occupation army and the old man was comforted by it at the end of his life when he had great debts: time went on and on, and released him. His name was Rembrandt van Rijn. When the girl was taken from the house, one could not talk about release, she went to the hell of the extermination camp. The house where the girl used to be in hiding can be visited and is named the "Anne Frank House". The grave of the old man can also be visited.

Although the organ is an old instrument – it was there even before Amadeus Mozart's father took an interest in it – it was originally exclusively for the rich, after that for the middle classes (eighteenth century). However only in the nineteenth century did it appear in the bars (as an instrument for dance music) and in the streets. After 1892, when the Italian Anselmo Gavioli invented the cardboard organ book, a kind of punched card system that did not require a lot of room and was not too heavy, the number of organs increased. (See the small organ on page 47). It made the organ easy to transport. These organs are still an odd but festive part of the Amsterdam street scene. The man with the penny-box (mansebek) is a "mansemaker", an old jargon-Yiddish name derived from the Hebrew word "maneh", meaning "mint".

Visitors to the Dutch capital often wonder why a great
number of Amsterdam inhabitants can tell rather
accurately from what year certain houses in the inner
city date. To begin with: the houses on the three circles
of canals all date after 1612, because before that year
those three canals did not even exist, neither did the
canal-houses. Not much from the old times has been
kept in the whole of the city. This has an obvious reason.
In the "Middle Ages" all houses were made of wood.
Because of the small space available within the fortress

the houses were very
narrow and had wooden
facades in a triangular
shape. The triangular
shape was maintained for a
while, until later, when
bricks were used. After
that the brick step facades
were in fashion, soon
followed by ornaments on
the steps, the so-called
"claw-bits". This step
facade was the forerunner
of the neck facade with its
very high middle bit.

Leidsegracht

The protuberances on the gables serve to hang a pulley-block, to lift or lower goods, merchandise in the old days, furniture nowadays. A great number of these premises did not only serve as living quarters, they were warehouses as well: there used to be a lot of trade on a small scale. The old fashioned vessel that just happened to be in the photograph, takes us back to the times when Amsterdam was situated on the shores of an inland sea (the "Zuiderzee" which later became the "IJsselmeer"). The entire city with all those canals used to be one harbour. That was possible because trade was done on a small scale. The trade expanded and became profitable when the tropics were explored in the sixteenth century.

A person who visits Amsterdam for the very first time, can easely get confused by the many different shapes of the facades. At first the Amsterdam houses were made out of wood, and in these times – the late Middle Ages – the so called stepped facades came about. Around 1650 the so called neck facades came into fashion, according to the first designs of architect Vingbooms. The neck facade is often seen with decorations which are full of fantasies, like figures of animals, flowers and even Greek Gods. The bell facade was derived from the neck facade (18th century). The decorations of the bell facade are on the lines of the silhouette, but often even more exuberant than the neck facade. During the 17th an 18th century cornices (mostly out of wood) were placed. These were raised in the middle to hide the old triangular rooftop. During the baroque period they became more luxurious, complete with balustrades and flower vases.

Stepped facade

Neck facade

Bell facade ▲ *Binnenkant*

One can not think about the Amsterdam history without remembering the stories of the lives of many refugees that found a safe haven in the Netherlands and especially in Amsterdam.

The ages would be able to tell hundreds of thousands of stories, often stories about persons who have remained unknown. When a Italian nobleman – his name was Giovanni Bartolotti – defected to tolerant Amsterdam for faith reasons, he did not remain unknown, not only because of his association with the at that time famous and rich Van den Heuvel family. On "Herengracht" numbers 170-172 one sees the "Bartolotti-house", that was built in 1620 by the famous architect Hendrick de Keyser under orders from Willem Van den Heuvel, who became the founder of an Italian bank called Bartolotti. With its magnificant interior architecture the house was a meeting place for all those promoting art and culture in the seventeenth century. It was meant to be a house, but later it was divided into two houses, and very well known Amsterdam families have lived here. Both parts have been marvellously restored in about 1970. The well-known musician Gustov Leonard wrote an elaborate history about the two houses – thus the original Bartolotti house. While writing the book he actually lived in one of the two houses.

The official numbering of houses in the Netherlands was started during the time of Napoleon. At that time the Dutch also had to choose a surname. All Dutch inhabitants were recorded in a registry-office. Before these governed times the people marked their houses not by number or name, but with a nice portrait, that was often sculptured in stone, a so called "stone-tablet". They were set into the facade, often in the centre of the facade above the first floor, but also often above the door, in the roof-cornice or other floors. If you keep looking up while sightseeing through Amsterdam, you will find hundreds of those tablets or plaques. Not all, by far, relate to the name or trade of the inhabitants concerned. On the corner of "Herengracht" and "Leidsegracht" for instance one can see a picture of the "Vier Heemskinderen". The ones that want to take it easy, can visit the "St. Luciensteeg" (between "Kalverstraat" and "Nieuwe Zijds Voorburgwal") where they can visit a kind of open air museum for stone-tablets.

Keizersgracht 123

The "Royal Historical Society" took the initiative to set a great number of these stone-tablets in the old walls of the former "Burgerweeshuis" (A home for orphans of citizens of Amsterdam). They were preserved during alterations. One can also find a collection in the facade of the "Begijnhof", as well as in the "St. Olofssteeg" near "Het Kolkje" and in the walls at the rear of the "Rijksmuseum". The houses were marked in different ways as well, for instance in all kinds of heraldry or with sculptures, like in the "House of Heads" (Keizersgracht 123) Jokes were permitted as well, like the mirror-image on the "Lindengracht". This tradition is still continuing here and there, like the plumber who screwed a tap onto the facade of his home.

The cities of which the street lay-out is a work of art, are scarce. It is an aesthetic pleasure – not only for the citizen of Amsterdam – to look at the map of the Amsterdam inner city, which is encircled by many majestic canals. In the middle, top of the photograph, is the Central Station dating from the nineteenth century, which blocked the view over the "IJ" – once the main water artery of the capital – for the pedestrians on "Damrak". This boulevard leads to the heart of the city, the "Dam" with the famous palace, behind which the "Paleisstraat" takes you to the "Westerkerk", with the much praised "Westertoren". In doing so you will have crossed the bridges of "Singel", "Herengracht", "Keizersgracht" and "Prinsengracht". This way the Amsterdam people can wander on this map, an event on every square inch, a new novel every minute.

There is no city in the world without graffiti. Amsterdam is no exception. While graffiti artists do not have an easy time in other cities, they are tolerated, maybe even stimulated, in Amsterdam. Because deep in his heart every Amsterdam citizen is a dauber, a real illegal, a colourful protester. An Amsterdam citizen does not bow to authority, on the contrary, he is always opposing the law. In kingdom, the capital is republican. Amsterdam has always been a city state within the State. Just like any other artist the unknown graffiti artist looks for his unknow twin. Response via the wall. There is plenty of it in Amsterdam. In secret. He has many twin brothers.

Because of new production and communication methods, many are unemployed. Thousands try to make use of their spare time by practising art. In the twilight between professionals and amateurs, between fame and anonymity, the pavement artists operate, the Johnny Romers and many others. They want to be recognised simply because they are there.

Pavement artistry in Kalverstraat

In the Netherlands, and especially in Amsterdam, art is practised more today than ever before. There are more novel writers, than fifty years ago, more poets, composers, entertaining musicians and more painters. Is this because of the the increase of leisure time? Everyone has a right to everything, and particularly the privilege to exhibit his kind of humour on a wall. Everyone has a right to express his feelings about life. The joy as a result of positive happenings in the world's politics (see on the right) is expressed by flowers. Flowers are abundant in Amsterdam. Maybe this is what visitors remember most: Amsterdam is a permanent "Keukenhof", the floral exhibition.

Flowers in "de Jordaan"

There is no Dutch livingroom without flowers. Not various plants in pots, but at least always one vase of cut flowers. Buying cut flowers is for a Dutch man or woman as common – even necessary – as buying bread. One easily notices the great number of flower stalls in the streets of Amsterdam. Daughters buy flowers for their mothers. Men coming home late buy roses for their wives. Everyone knows where to buy them, each has a favourite stall. The florist is his friend.

Singel

Flower Stall in Utrechtsestraat

As for housing quarters Amsterdam is an extremely paradoxical city. In spite of all energetic efforts, the nice ideas about town- and areaplanning, the fresh vision on better housing with the best of hygienic facilities, and in spite of the great and good intentions, one still has not managed to overcome the lack of living accommodation.

After the First World War, when there was a crisis in the building trade that had long after-effects, it was difficult to build sufficient houses. After 1945, thus after World War II, there was an even greater need, because of the results of the war. Though building was started on the outskirts of the city, the situation in the inner city was desperate until

the eighties, because meantime the average size of a family changed and many a young person preferred to live alone or in a commune, the ideal solution always was in the offing.

Large groups of "squatters" took the law into their own hands and occupied different empty premises, that often were not even meant to be living quarters, like dismantled factories or old offices. The above left photograph shows the (fictitious) names on the door of illegal occupied premises, where many youngsters at least have a roof over their head, though in rather dirty conditions.

Over 700.000 people live in the city now. That number used to be higher, but many people were forced to find room in the spaces of the countryside, where during the last decades small sleepy towns have been revived and where new communities have been built, like in the new polders of the "IJsselmeer". Meantime there is a new trend to go back to the city: many prefer to live in the capital. This is no longer a problem for people with the means. Living in old, superfluous warehouses that have been restored, became so popular that the new style of gables has been adapted for brandnew houses.

Amsterdam has hundreds of bridges. Some sources talk about more than 600, but that includes bridges that can not be recognised as such. Nevertheless, there is no other city in the world that has so many bridges. The original oldest bridges have not been preserved. The oldest, still existing bridge is the "Torensluis", dating from 1648. If one uses a word like "Torensluis" (Tower-lock) one need not necessarily think of an actual lock: in the days gone by an Amsterdam local meant a bridge made out of stone or brick when using the word "lock".

The wooden structure (above) spanning the "Amstel" river is not a "lock" in Amsterdam language, but is commonly called "bridge" and rather uncommonly "the Skinny Bridge". During the last quarter of the seventeenth century there was a small foot-bridge spanning the broad waters. Since then it has been changed, dismantled and reconstructed and even during this century, in 1929, the bridge was dismantled once again. Fortunately the "Skinny Bridge" then was rebuilt as a wooden double drawbridge, improving the view on the Amstel river.

Skinny Bridge

Many visitors that come to Amsterdam, would very much like to see a diamond factory. This is still possible. There are well organised excursions to factories with old (fortunately also with young) diamond cutters, who are part scientist and part artist. In those enterprises one can often buy – for special prices – the fascinating sparkling stones, set in a ring, a brooch or necklace. The diamond industry was a trend setter for the growth, the spirit and the festivity of Amsterdam. At the beginning of this century, when Amsterdam was very prosperous, the number of workers in the diamond industry increased to ten thousand.

In those old days there was a lot of competition from Antwerp – also a real diamond city – but Amsterdam boasted many more real craftsmen and was remarkably better organised.

The Amsterdam diamond cutters earned well, enjoyed politics, reading and art (many of them love opera). Their money and love for culture stimulated the city's flourish.
The depression of the thirties however caused a setback and World War II nearly ended the amazing, delicate industry.

Diamond sawing machine

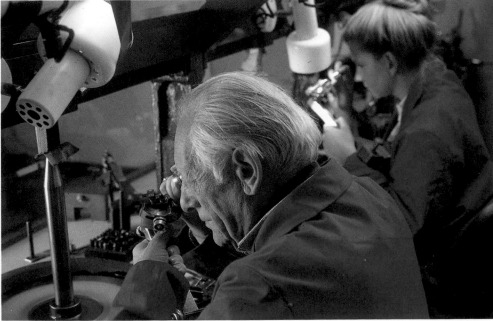

But like a miracle, some diamond factories came to life again in spite of competition from Antwerp, that was not so badly hit. They give that peculiar, extra sparkle to the Amsterdam reputation.

Photographs courtesy of "Coster Diamonds" Museumplein"

During the previous century there was a man by the name of Sinckel who owned a shop were one could buy everything: hats and caps and corsets. Now the whole of Amsterdam is one enormous Sinckel shop, where one can buy anything, believe it or not – in the big department stores, like the "Bijenkorf" (Beehive) and in exclusive fashion shop streets (the P.C. Hooftstraat or Beethovenstraat) for instance, special antique areas (the Spiegelstraat area) working class areas with cheaper shops with electronic equipment or low budget gentlemen's clothes, or naughty lingerie (Kinkerstraat, Jan Evertsenstraat and Vijzelstraat).

In the Chinese quarters (Zeedijk area) you will find a great variety of Asian food and in the "Jordaan" area there is such an enormous choice of different articles (see photograph above) that we advise you to have a look yourself.

"Museumboat"

The person that wants to take it easy, and see as many museums as possible in one day, in a comfortable way, should take the "Museumboat", a kind of water-tram that goes from one museum to the other (above – in front of the "Rijksmuseum"). You can get off where you wish, stay as long as you like, take the next boat, etc. Nothing beats the Amsterdam way.

Private transport along the canal

◀ *Watertaxi*

▼ *"Canal Bikes"*

"Canal Bus"

While travelling on the water – by watertaxi for example – one can meet strange waterbirds, sportive Amsterdam people, that make use of their rights, since the Amsterdam waters are free and entirely public. If you want to be "homo ludens", and want to boat on your own, you can hire a water-bike. For groups you can also hire special boats. You can even dine on board. One need not organise this: in the evening there are trips through the canals with wine and a meal by candlelight.

The Amsterdam people have been drinking beer for a long time, because – so one claims – the quality of the drinking water was not reliable: beer has always been pure. That was a good excuse anyhow! Do not get upset, there is nothing wrong with the Amsterdam drinking water now. The Dutch keep their water well under control. Especially the waters of the sea and rivers. Now we are talking about dikes and water levels. To measure the latter, the entire nation uses an old Amsterdam standard, the so called "Amsterdams Peil", that dates from the time (before 1932) when Amsterdam was open to the sea. In the modern Amsterdam town-hall a monument has been erected to "Amsterdam Peil", a splendid measuring glass, several meters tall, which shows all different Dutch water levels. The higher one reads the glass, the more dangerous the situation is. With beer it works just the other way. The words "Brown cafe" have a certain meaning in the whole of the Netherlands. They are dark, often old fashioned rooms, where alcohol is consumed. They can be compared to the English pubs, that also really are public living rooms. However, the Dutch brown cafe's are "gezellig", and that is a special word as well.

Amsterdam Measure in Stopera building

Cafe Hoppe on Spui

"Gezellig" is typical Dutch and means "intimate", "with each other" and especially it stands for "away from everyday duties". The largest number of brown cafe's is in Amsterdam; you will find dozens and dozens of them, in nearly every quarter, especially in the oldest areas. As a matter of fact, they form one of the many attractions of Amsterdam, because they maintained their position in a world that tends to uniformity. They are small bastions against the

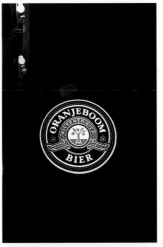

problems of the big world, and each of them is unique: a brown cafe is only perfect when it has character of its own.

Although each brown cafe has a large variety of "spirits" to offer, mostly beer is served at the bar. For a long time the tradition was that a brown cafe only had one kind of beer for sale, the brand of the brewery that financially supported it. These times are almost over. In the world of beer the battle against uniformity has been won. Each cafe owner is proud of the variety of special beers from all over Europe, and of which each kind has an unmistakable speciality.

Cafe Nol in Westerstraat in "Jordaan"

Zuiderkerk

▲ *Binnenkant*

KrommeWaal ▲
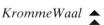

Amsterdam is a poetric city in many aspects, especially in winter, when everything is clear under a freezing blue sky and when after a couple of frosty nights a new world opens up for the skating-enthousiast. If there is snow as well everything is even more beautiful. The city offers itself so to speak to the first wood sculpturer or etcher. The Dutch capital counts hundreds of them: all artists who consider themselves too good or great for the province – whatever that may be – and sooner or later move to the capital to try their luck there. The same goes for writers and poets and a great number of musicians. Because "Amsterdam has it", to use a slogan used only a few years ago.

A lot changed in Amsterdam between the beginning of industrialisation of the Netherlands (around 1860) and the beginning of World War I. Thousands of people from the country moved to the capital to work in the factories there. The traffic by horse and carriage increased enormously, canals were filled in, breaches were made in the city, bridges were built, and streetlights were introduced everywhere. That happened during the turn of the century, the time of "Jugendstil". That's why one can still see beautiful examples of that romantic style on many street lights.

Gelderse kade

The style of the red lights is an entirely different matter. Contrary to foreigners the Dutch have no problem with the so-called "red light districts", with their quarters for "paid love". How does one explain the great tolerance of the Dutch, and especially the Amsterdam population? Some say, this is the consequence of the way one earns a living in Amsterdam, partly earned by commerce. Amsterdam became important through the international traffic of goods. One had to, and still has – to trade with many nations, many religions, many skin colours and many preferences. Even religious people, look more relatively at the world on Mondays than on Sundays. The subject is an old one. In many a harbour town, bold ladies behind red lights, are permitted, often connive. In Amsterdam those ladies sit at the windows, quite openly and nobody objects!

Stopera

From the early months of summer until the early autumn Amsterdam is a fairly-like city, because for years and years now it has been the tradition to illuminate the inner city. Along the old river "Amstel" from which Amsterdam derives its name, is the most beautiful part on a quiet summer's evening. It is only a few minutes walk from the townhall-music theatre buildings to the old, famous squares called after Rembrandt and Thorbecke. Some establishments on Thorbecke Square and the larger adjoining Rembrandt Square like to identify themselves with the Paris atmosphere on Place Pigalle. The decent citizen thinks of them in an aroma of adventure and tolerable naughtiness. More than a century ago there was an entirely different smell, the smell of Dutch butter and cheese. Then, those squares were called Butter and Cheese market. There are cities, like Venice for instance, that can be best visited in the quiet season, when there are not many people about. Why? Because they are museums in themselves, splendid remainders of the past. Old, historic Amsterdam on the contrary is a living city with modern ways of existance. Outwith the tourist season it is a bustling city. Always. The bustling elements of toerism magnify the vital aspects of Amsterdam.

Carre theatre and
Skinny Bridge

They add attractive
aspects. The thousands,
hundreds of thousands of
tourists in Amsterdam feel
at home at once, because
they feel they are welcome.

Rembrandtsplein

The Amsterdam people love their tourists, because they
make Amsterdam even more beautiful during summer.
Especially in the evenings. The inner city of Amsterdam
is illuminated in a fairly-like way, mainly for the tourists.

Herengracht

The Amsterdam people enjoy it as well. There is no town for walking like Amsterdam. Tourists and citizens wander together along the canals, along the "Amstel" and along the side canals like the "Reguliersgracht".

◀ *Bartolottihouse* *Minttower*

Panorama of the Amstel with Skinny Bridge

Citizens and foreigners alike experience the tale of a real, human city, that honours the splendid remains of a distant, very rich past. Two incomparable wealths compete, the gold of the old sailing trade created a different prosperity than the scientific thinking of our technical era. However, in historical terms the one wealth is associated with the other.

Reguliersgracht

Although the first railroad – between Haarlem and Amsterdam – was opened in 1839, it was not until 1870 before one could boast of a complete national system that had good connections with the adjoining countries. The reason was that the Netherlands already had a splendid transport system in the nineteenth century by way of the countless canals and rivers. Transport was by means of tow-boat, running on a schedule, with good connections, and thus one could travel through the country in a few days without getting too tired.

A'dam-Sloterdijk Station

The water competed with the railways in yet a different way: the country with its many waterways needed many railway bridges, sometimes very long ones, like the one that spans the river "Hollands Diep". This one kilometer long bridge was completed during the seventies of the past century. This completed the rail connection with Paris. Neutral Holland became part of Europe again. The appearance of the motorcar made it very difficult for the railways after World War II, however, in the Netherlands the train is flourishing more than ever, mainly owing to its efficiency. There is an intercity train from Amsterdam at least once every half our to all main towns in the Netherlands. They run on the dot. Within a few hours one can reach a remote destination without having to reserve a seat. In the Netherlands one can see the triumph of the efficiency expressed in new functional stations.

After World War II, everywhere round Amsterdam new quarters were built. In the beginning first and foremost for living purposes.

It took a long time to make a decision about the destiny of the old heart of Amsterdam, that admittedly had suffered because of the war, but had kept its character of ages past. Would one have to opt for high buildings in the old city in these evolving times? One can notice this hesitance on the Amsterdam Frederiksplein, where the twin buildings of

the Netherland Bank have been erected (not shown here). Finally the choice was made in favour of a trade center in the outskirts of the city, in the south-east.

Quite different from Rotterdam thus, where on the empty spaces of the destroyed inner city, impressive sky-scrapers of glass have been built, and still are being built in the heart of the city. Amsterdam on the contrary expands outwith the periphery. After a very large and high-rise living area – de Bijlmer – was built, and later a gigantic ultra-modern hospital – the Amsterdam Medical Centre – the large enterprises came as well. Most of them were built of glass, entirely according to the Bauhaus glory. Fortunately one can also see exceptions, like the castle-like bank (top left) that is really typical of Amsterdam, the style is the echo of the sturdy determination of the twenties, when in the capital the so-called Amsterdam School was created, an architectural ideology.

Skyline of office area south-east Amsterdam

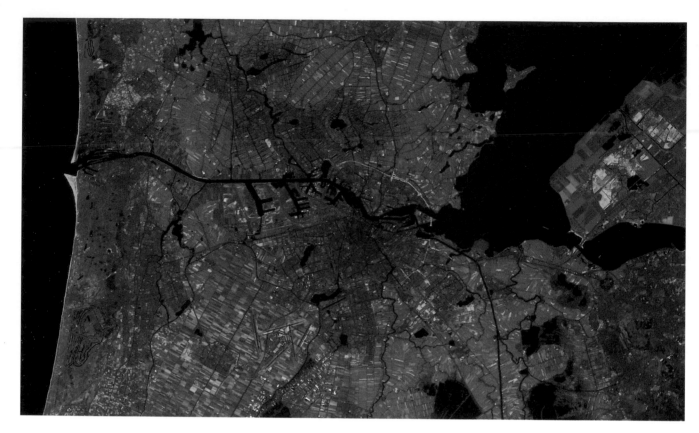

We conclude this book with a last impression of
Amsterdam, that was realised through the new
techniques of satellite pictures. One can clearly
distinguish the circled shape of the canals. But to get a
taste of the mood, to admire the beauty of Amsterdam,
we advise you to pay a visit to this city. Amsterdam
welcomes you, throughout the year.